Acknowledgements

IƟ161755

To my husband Durvin, and my daughter Sheneen, thank you for your love and endless support. To my Instructors Ann Maree W-Brown, Ph. D and Bishop Ephraim Jackson, Ph. D, thank you for your support.

To God be the Glory!

Encouragement and Prayer from Psalm 1 – 10

(King James Version)

By Shelia Soares

Psalm 1

The Blessed Man

The Psalmist is saying that God's blessings will be upon that man whose lifestyle is not patterned according to the ungodly man. His life is not a barrier or stumbling block to those who are lost in their sins, and he also does not keep company with skeptics. This man delights in the Word of God and ponders it continuously.

The promises of God to this godly man are mentioned in verse three. He shall flourish like a tree that is planted by the rivers and shall be successful in whatever he does in due season. It went on to speak of the end of the ungodly man; he shall perish. The ungodly man shall not stand in the congregation where the righteous will be rewarded, but shall utterly perish.

Notes:

Psalm 2

Title: *Thou Art My Son*

The Psalmist asked a question in verse one of Psalm two: Why are the Gentiles filled with anger and the thoughts of the people empty? Verse two stated that the rulers of the earth formed a coalition against God the Father and His Son Jesus, who is the Anointed One. Verse three continues to state that the world does not want the Lord to rule over them, so they purposed in their hearts to break all ties with the Lord.

In verse four of the same chapter, the Psalmist wrote of the exalted position of The Lord. He that sitteth in the heavens shall laugh. The Lord shall laugh at their folly and will ridicule them. Verse five speaks of the wrath of God coming upon them and distress will be upon them. Verse six speaks of the Lord installing His king to rule in Jerusalem. In Verse seven, the word will be declared throughout the earth that Jesus Christ is the only begotten Son of God.

In verse eight, the Psalmist spoke of the Gentiles becoming an inheritance of the Lord; this happens through the promised Messiah who came to make Jews and Gentiles one in Christ Jesus through His blood. Verse nine declares that the Lord shall rule with a rod of iron, and the fierceness of His anger shall be unto those who have rejected Him.

Verse ten is calling all the rulers of the earth to be wise and take heed to the instructions of the Lord; for whatever he says He will do; it must come to pass.

Verse eleven is a reminder to serve the Lord in holy reverence and celebrate in awe of who He is.

Verse twelve reminds us to worship the Lord Jesus who is the Son of God, lest he be angry with us and we stray from His way. A blessing is pronounced upon all those who put their trust in Jesus.

Notes:

Psalm 3

Title: *I Will Not Be Afraid*

Lord, there is trouble all around me; my enemies have increased. Many believe that I am in a helpless situation.

But You, O God, are my protector, my place of honor and You keep me above shame.

I prayed to You O Lord, and You answered me out of Your exalted place.

I slept in peace, and I am awake because of Your mercies that sustain me.

I will be brave, even though there is an abundance of enemies surrounding me.

Show Yourself strong on my behalf, Oh God, save me; strike my enemies, I pray, and break down their defenses.

Deliverance comes only from You, Oh God. Your favor is upon your people.

Notes:

Psalm 4

Title: *Hear Me When I Call*

The Psalmist in verse one cried out to the Lord in prayer, asking the Lord to relieve him of his distress and to have mercy and be attentive to his prayer.

Verse two is a rebuke to humanity for turning the glory of the Lord into shameful living and seeking after the temporal things in life. Verse three is a reminder that the Lord has consecrated him that is godly unto Himself, and the Lord will hear the prayer of His sanctified people.

Verse four reminds us to be in awe of who God is and to live a sinless life. Meditate in your heart when laying upon your bed and be confident in who God is.

Verse five reminds us to worship God and put our trust in Him.

Verse six questions who will show goodness to God's people. He asked the Lord to illuminate the path of His people.

Verse seven speaks of the joy that the Lord has placed in his heart which is more than the harvest of their corn and wine.

Verse eight speaks of the confidence that the psalmist has in the Lord that he will sleep in peace because the Lord is his place of safety.

Notes:

Psalm 5

Title: *In the Morning*

Listen to my prayer, Oh Lord, and give attention to the thoughts of my heart. Attend unto the voice of my cry, Oh God my King. In the morning, I will pray unto thee O Lord, and I will look up to You from where comes my help.

You take no pleasure in the deeds of the wicked for You are a Holy God. The foolish shall not approach Your throne; You hate all evil. You will destroy them that speak lies, and You hate murderers and deceivers.

As for me, I will approach your throne with worship because You are a God of great mercy, and Your name is to be revered. Lead me, O Lord, in Your righteous pathway because of mine enemies. Make the way clear before me.

My enemies are unfaithful in their walk and they conceive only wickedness and the words from their mouth are deceptive. Bring destruction on them, Oh God; let their own words condemn them because they have rebelled against You.

May all those that trust in You rejoice because You are our defender. May all those that trust in Thy name be filled with joy. For You, Oh Lord, will bring blessing and divine favor to Your people. You will surround them with Your protection.

Notes:

Psalm 6

Title: *The Lord Hath Heard*

Oh Lord, don't scold me when You are angry, and please do not discipline me when You are displeased.

Be merciful to me, Oh Lord, for I am weak; bring healing to my inner man, for I am tormented.

My soul is very troubled in me. How long Oh Lord before you respond to me. Return, Oh Lord, rescue my soul and deliver me according to thy lovingkindness. When I die, Oh Lord, I cannot remember thee; who can utter thanksgiving to you from the grave?

I am becoming faint with all my lamentation. My bed is soaked with the tears that I cried throughout the night. Grief has consumed me. I look unhealthy because of my sadness. My countenance appears old because of the pressure from mine enemies.

I will speak to my enemies and say "depart from me you iniquity workers for the Lord has heard my cry and will avenge my enemies."

With confidence I will say that the Lord hath heard my petitions and has attended to my prayer.

I will declare that all my enemies will come to shame and great trouble will come upon them suddenly.

Notes:

Psalm 7

Title: *In Thee Do I Put My Trust*

Oh Lord my God, my confidence is in You. Rescue me from my persecutors; please deliver me, Oh God, or else the enemy will tear my soul in pieces like a lion does to its prey, if You don't come to my rescue.

Oh Lord my God, if I have done wickedness, if my hands are soiled with iniquity, please forgive me.

If I have rewarded evil for good, if I have delivered him that was at peace with me and call him my enemy, I am wrong Oh Lord.

Let the enemy take revenge upon me, if I am wrong. Oh God, make me to trust in You, even if I don't understand, for You are a just God.

Arise Oh Lord, in Thy Holy anger; show Yourself strong on my behalf because of the fury of mine enemies; act on my behalf for You are the righteous judge.

The congregation of the people shall surround Thee; for their sakes, Oh God, glorify Thyself.

The Lord shall try the people. Examine me, Oh Lord, according to Your righteous judgement, and see if I am a man of integrity.

Let the iniquity of the wicked come to an end and affirm the upright, for You are a righteous God who examines the hearts and minds.

You are my defense, Oh Lord, who saves the righteous.

God You are a just judge, and You are angry with the wicked every day.

If the wicked do not turn, He will sharpen His sword and make His bow ready for war. Look and see the wicked plots that he has conceived and the lies and mischief that he had produced.

He shall dig a pit and fall in it; the evil that he conceived shall devour him.

I will praise You, Oh Lord, for You are a righteous God. I will sing praise to your exalted name, Oh Lord.

Notes:

Psalm 8

Title: *How Excellent Is Thy Name*

Oh Lord, our master, how excellent is Your name in all the earth; the heavens declare Your majesty.

Out of the mouth of children Your praise is perfected, because of Your enemies. You still the voice of the enemy and the avenger.

When I think about Your heavens and the work of Your hands, the moon and the stars that You put in place.

What is man that You take thought of him? And the son of man that you visit him.

You have made him in human form and have covered him with Your power and majesty. You have given him authority and government over the works of Your hands. Everything is subjected to him. All the beast of the field, and fowls of the air, and all the sea creatures. Oh Lord, Our Lord, Your name is excellent in all the earth.

Notes:

Psalm 9

Title: *With My Whole Heart*

I will praise Thee, Oh Lord, with all my heart. I will tell of your marvelous works.

Because I am in fellowship with You Oh God, gladness and rejoicing is in my heart, so I will sing praises to your great name O most high God.

When my enemies come after me, they shall fall and be destroyed because of the power of Your Holy presence.

You are the righteous judge that sits on Your throne and have maintained my right and cause.

You have disciplined the sinner and have destroyed the wicked; You have blot out their names forever.

Utter destruction has come to the enemy; their cities are become desolate, and every memory of them has perished.

You, Oh God, shall endure forever. Your throne is set up for justice.

You shall judge the world in righteous judgement. You will minister Your righteous justice to the people.

You, Oh Lord, will be a safe place for those that are oppressed; a refuge in the times of trials.

The people that know Your name, Oh God, will put their confidence in You. For You, Oh Lord, will never turn away from those who seek after You.

Sing praises to the Lord whose dwelling place is Zion. Speak of His mighty works among the people.

When He makes inquiry for destruction, He remembers the cry of the humble.

Be merciful to me, Oh Lord; take thought of the trouble that I am going through because of my enemies. You are the one that rescues my soul from death.

That I may declare Your honor and praise in Jerusalem, I will be joyful because You rescue me.

The sinners have fallen in the pit that they dig; the net that they hid to ensnare me, their own feet are caught in it.

You are known, Oh Lord, for Your righteous justice that you execute, and the wicked has fallen into his own trap.

The wicked and the ungodly nations shall be thrown into hell.

For the needy You will not forget, and the expectation of the poor shall come to pass.

Arise Oh Lord, let not the wicked prevail; let Your judgement come upon the sinners. Put fear upon them, Oh Lord, so that the nations will know that they are mere men.

Notes:

Psalm 10

Title: *Thou Hast Seen, Thou Hast Heard*

Why are You so far from me O Lord? Why are You hiding Yourself from me in the time of my troubles?

The wicked in their lofty thinking and their evil ways are persecuting the poor. They cause them to be ensnared in their evil plots. The wicked boasts of what his evil heart conspires and favors the covetous man whom You disgust.

The wicked heart is filled with pride so he will not seek after You, Oh God. He does not consider You in anything that he does. The ways of the wicked are always injurious; he does not seek Your righteous justice; he is insulting to all who opposes him. He has said in his heart that nothing can move him and that no calamity can come his way.

His mouth is filled with cursing, lying, and fraud; his tongue makes mischief and speaks empty words. He lurks in the secret corners of the villages from which he commits his murderous acts against the innocent and secretly set against the poor.

He lies in wait like a lion awaiting its prey; he lies in wait to catch the poor. He catches the weak when he draws him into his net. He pretends to be humble that the poor may fall into his trap.

The wicked believes in his heart that You have forgotten, Oh Lord. He said that You have hidden Your face and does not take notice of his evil ways.

Arise, Oh Lord, and avenge the enemy; do not forget the humble, Oh Lord.

For what reason does the wicked disrespect Your name, Oh Lord? He believes in his heart that You do not require reverence from Your creation.

You have seen the mischief and the spite that is done to the poor; avenge the enemy according to his evil work, for You are the helper of the fatherless. Destroy the source of the wicked deeds of the enemy; search thoroughly until all his evil ways are destroyed.

The Lord is King forever and ever; the sinners are perished from out of His land. Lord You have heard the prayer of the humble, and You will establish their hearts. You will incline Your ears to hear the cry of the humble.

You bring justice to the fatherless and the oppressed, so that the enemy can cause no more oppression.

Notes:

www.ingramcontent.com/pod-product-compliance
Lightning Source LLC
Chambersburg PA
CBHW041805040426
42448CB00001B/46

* 9 7 8 0 6 9 2 8 7 9 8 4 9 *